Killing Law Enforcement

From within the ranks

By

Samantha Smith

&

Nicholas Ruggiero

All rights reserved. No part of this publication may be reproduced, distributed, or transmitted in any form or by any means, including photocopying, recording, or other electronic or mechanical methods, without the prior written permission of the publisher, except in the case of brief quotations embodied in critical reviews and certain other noncommercial uses permitted by copyright law.

Dedications

This book is dedicated to the men and women who fight every day with the internal politics within their agency and still go out and do the job flawlessly.

To my wife, another book.. These dedications never get hard for me because your love and support never waivers. You're always there to point me in the right direction.

To my daughters. I always thought my legacy was to run after criminals and be Batman. It's these books that I write to guide the next generation of law enforcement. Something for you to be proud of.

Mike, Lisa, Michael, and Joe, love you guys!

Ernie, Dennis, John, Ed, Logan, Chad, Dave, and Mike thank you for always being there.

Nick

This book is dedicated to the first responders who battle every day not only in our communities to keep us safe but from within to protect themselves and their progress.
To the marginalized voices who are fighting to be heard!

To my wife, Olga, for your love and support is a constant that allows me to serve our community and continue to be a voice for those who are unable.

To my kiddos Ethan, Innessa, and Chris for making me feel like a superhero and allowing me to help guide you on your paths to leave a positive legacy in this World.

Lee, Kat, Mom, Kev, and Dad for always being in my corner, love you all!

Sam

Nicholas Ruggiero

Blood in the water. That's all it takes for some within our profession to pounce and go for the kill. Within our profession, our culture has always been one of getting ahead by any means and the team comes later if at all.

We see this a lot within smaller police departments. That doesn't mean that it doesn't happen in the larger departments, it just means it's really prevalent in a smaller department.

In the academy, the instructors are very focused on instilling the core values of law enforcement and turning out the best product. Yes, I said product. You are a product for your agency. They have invested a great deal of money into you before you even walk across the stage and take the oath. While you're in the academy, instructors, command staff, and human resources are discussing what time of product you are or will be. Officers within your department are hearing about what type of product you'll be and forming opinions on you without you even working a shift.

Field training officers (FTO's) meet after your graduation and are briefed on each of you. Before they even take you in the cruiser for your first shift they have pre-judged your product. They have already organized their training style to what they've heard. Your minor mistakes will be analyzed and "the benefit of the doubt" will be based on what the FTO's have been briefed on.

Sound familiar? This happens in every department and sets the stage for what Samantha and I will discuss in this book.

We have created a culture within our profession that is neither professional nor sustainable any longer in law enforcement. Our culture needs to change because we've reached a point where the war on police is not only from the anti-police movement but from within.

Our recruitment within the profession has also taken a major hit because of pay, benefits, and public opinion on the profession of being a police officer. Then when we hire new officers they leave within three years because of the culture within the agency. If they stay it takes a mental toll on officers dealing with the internal politics and watching your back from fellow officers.

The culture is what's killing us from within. The culture is what's contributing to high suicide rates within law enforcement. The culture can be changed but must be done right. It starts from the top of the agency. The Chief or Sheriff needs to own the bad culture.

They must identify what bad culture lurks within the organization. Identify clicks and the leaders of these clicks. We all have them, we all have that group within our agencies that thrives on misery and drama.

In my old department, we had a "click" led by a Lieutenant stuck in high school. This one person was the center of every gossip or disbursement of someone's internal investigation without the investigation being over which was odd. This person created an atmosphere of favoritism and retaliation if you weren't in "the club". The people she surrounded herself with weren't loyal, they were in fear. The fear of being on the outs and not getting a promotion or assignment to a special unit. This person wore this title as a badge of honor and was rewarded time after time by upper command yet every group or unit she supervised turned into a disaster. Moral was always horrible and great officers left the agency because of her bullying and style of management.

This was not something that was hidden or in the shadows, it was well known and still is within the agency. Someone like this is an easy fix to change the culture within the agency. I like to call it "Clipping the wings". Some birds don't deserve to fly free in the wild, some birds belong in a spare room in the house in a cage on display with their wings clipped and ability to fly hindered.

This wasn't the only example within my old agency. We had a dictator, someone I referred to in my first book as a "Positional equity leader". This person was toxic and one of the most dangerous kinds of leaders/managers. For years this person was able to move up the chain of command through fear and intimidation. His ability to destroy your morale or retaliate against you for not agreeing with him or not executing one of his unlawful commands was unparalleled. In one instance when I was a Sergeant this commander ordered me to write up an officer before his internal investigation was completed. I refused and paid the price for three years. During meetings, this commander would single me out or behind closed doors prevent me from supervising specialized units. This commander was a coward and as I said before, he led with fear and intimidation. The thing with that type of leadership is fear will only last so long, and eventually, someone will come along to clip those wings.

These are a couple of examples of poor law enforcement leadership. I'm sure as you read this some of your own poor leadership comes to mind. You're not alone by a long shot.

That's why we have a culture problem within law enforcement. Because these two don't even scratch the surface of what's out there. We have paper leadership in a rainstorm... The past two years within law enforcement have exposed some of the worst leadership within agencies across the country.

COVID changed policing dramatically and the leadership within law enforcement wasn't prepared for it. These are people who came up the ranks with the only requirement was to keep the ship heading north and don't hit an iceberg. They were never tested in adaptability, crisis management, or forward-thinking. Instead of recognizing this and acknowledging that you don't know what you don't know, they pressed forward with "fake it till you make it". The problem with that is at the same time a major shift with support of law enforcement happened. The public had turned on our cops and for the first time in a long time, the trust from the public was strained.

These dinosaur commanders were lost. They couldn't adapt to the change so they did what they do best and what they were comfortable with. They turned their attention inward to the rank and file. Commanders heard that the police are bad and change needs to happen. They walked with the anti-police movements got on one knee and agreed. "Those police officers do need to be held accountable!". So what did the commanders of these agencies do? They started documenting every little thing. They started to lose reality and started to drop a sledgehammer down every citizen complaint, every cruiser accident, and every officer was guilty until never.

Morale started to plummet. Suicides within law enforcement started to tick up above the line of duty deaths. Officers started to stop working or leave the profession altogether. Crime started to skyrocket with part one crimes spiking because proactive policing was discouraged by these same commanders.

As all of this was going on COVID started to effecting law enforcement. Exposures led to COVID positive cases within the ranks across the country. Faced with extreme staffing issues these commanders made bad decisions worse by treating exposed officers like products again. They bullied COVID-positive officers into working anyway or restricted duty. These officers felt dehumanized and like cattle. Chaos within the ranks turned loyal police officers into punch in and punch out drones.

Even while this was going on most command staff didn't stop and ask the rank and file how to fix the problem. Instead, they invoked "the beatings will continue till morale gets better".

Agencies across the country were/are in critical staffing levels. Recruitment at an all-time low they turned to lower some standards to put asses in seats at the academies. The problem was that now most academies turned to hybrid education because of COVID. Virtual police academy. Yes, you read that right. Recruits were being taught virtually to become law enforcement officers.

Remember I told you about being a product? Now we have a whole generation of Amazon cops. These recruits upon completion of the police academy went into agencies with a major disadvantage and were not very well respected. To make matters worse, FTO's couldn't field train in some cases because of COVID restrictions or being discouraged to do proactive policing.

So what's the solution? How do we change our culture, restore trust with the public, and recruit the next generation of law enforcement? The solution is within the problem in law enforcement.

The first step is acknowledging that we have a problem within our profession. This is the hardest step for a lot of poor leaders within law enforcement. It takes a lot to stand in front of your troops and say, "This isn't working, and I'm the reason". I know a lot of leaders in law enforcement agencies that have done just that, allowed themselves to be vulnerable and judged. This had a tremendous effect on their agency. The level of trust the rank and file had in them after that vulnerability was something they didn't expect.

Being the leader of a law enforcement agency is more than wearing a bunch of stars or an eagle. It's more than having your name on the door. You not only took an oath to protect the citizens of your jurisdiction, but you took an unspoken oath to serve and protect your troops.

This protection sometimes comes at a major cost. Sometimes it means sacrificing your own career to stand up for what's right, even in the biggest adversity. When advisors and politicians are telling you to take someone down, it's your duty to build them up. When Internal Investigations within your agency complete an investigation and the scales are swayed and suspect, it's your duty to look into it and see the alternate motives and "clicks". When it's time to render punishment, be consistent, be fair, and most of all be a human. Your decisions or lack of decisions have the ability to affect that officer's life in a way that you can't believe. A good officer knows when they fucked up, a bad officer will bargain or come up with excuses. Recognize the difference.

After the chief can recognize failure comes the realization that for the next few years within our profession we must foster a guardian mindset.

I spent almost my entire career in community policing. This role was ridiculed by my peers, commanders, and in some instances the Chief. While my team was out playing baseball with kids or fostering relationships with criminals officers and commanders within my old agency were making fun. After a community event, it wasn't uncommon to come back to my office and find a picture of me and my team altered with disparaging remarks about community policing. I would tear them down and keep them from my unit because I wanted to shield them from the negativity. I knew what they were doing was putting money in the social bank. These same idiots that were making fun of us were the ones that one day would ask to make a withdrawal from our social bank for doing some dumb shit.

I tell you this not to get your sympathy or point out the shortcoming of our old agency, but to point out that the mindset was the more arrests I make the more the public will respect us, and the safer we will be. To some extent that is correct. Criminals need to be locked up, the wicked need to be held accountable. What you need to realize is that the relationships you foster with the public doing community policing pay you back in dividends. This not only fixes your community relations issues but it plants future recruitment seeds. Kids that I built relationships with while doing community policing are now pursuing careers within law enforcement.

If you don't infiltrate the teenagers now, you will never have trust in the future. If your department doesn't have a teen law enforcement academy, get one!

A teen law enforcement academy is an outstanding way for you to partner with the youth while changing the culture within your agency. If every interaction your officers have with teens is in an adversarial way then that bias will carry on.

Departments need to steer away from this hierarchy chart.

We can all agree that we serve the public as one of our main roles, but in order to do that, you must be in the very best you. The current setup in almost every law enforcement agency is in this chart. Officer wellness is at the very bottom. Your department's policy and liability far exceed officers' mental health. This is a recipe for disaster. If your officers aren't at their peak mental health or fitness for duty, the chances of them adhering to department policy or giving two shits about liability is slim to none.

Not many departments are willing to shake it up or change the hierarchy chart to this:

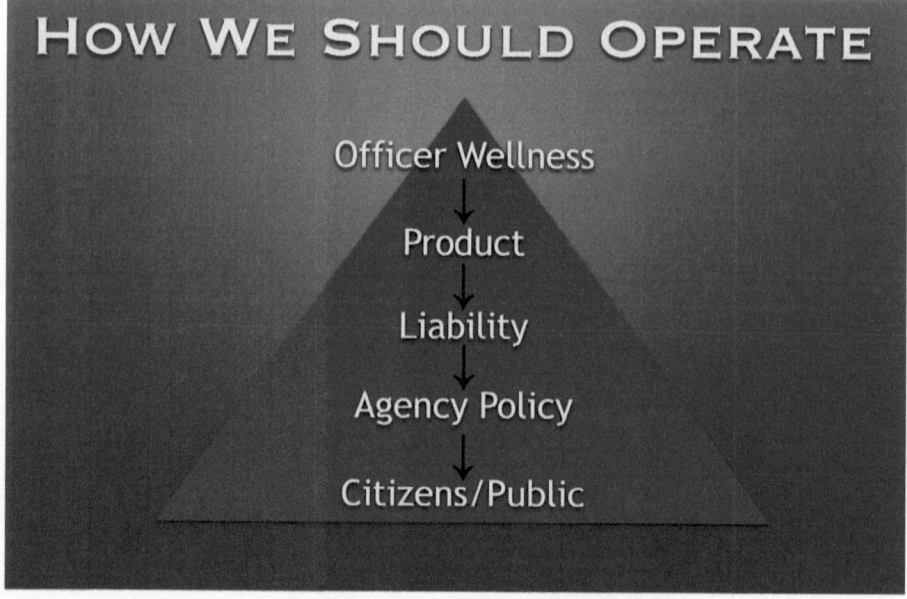

Officer wellness MUST be at the top. I don't care if you're the toughest cop kicking indoors or the happiest cop skipping to work every shift. If your mental health is shit, your product is shit. I've seen it time and time again as a Sergeant, officers wrapped up in dumb shit because of being burnt.

We must operate at this level. The public can't be served if our house isn't in order.

This pyramid comes with a lot of controversies. The anti-police and extreme "reformists" will pounce on this as a way to show that law enforcement thinks less of the public it serves. The idiocy of that thought process is hypocritical. The anti-police and reformists want change in law enforcement. They want the practices of the past changed and policies changed to better serve the community. What they don't realize is the same dinosaurs have been in charge of law enforcement for decades and just keep getting passed around from agency to agency like a peace pipe. The same bad decisions and bad policies enacted by under-qualified and un-tested "leaders" move from police department to police department without even a revision.

The bad policies that have gotten law enforcement into trouble or into trick bags are never written by the officer on the street pushing a police cruiser. They are birth in a conference room, commander's office, or part of some academic paper a commander is writing to get to the next level. These policies are very rarely birthed by patrol committees and if they are by the time the committee's findings make it up the chain of command it's nothing like the originally designed policy.

The reason is driven by fear and control. We have poor leaders so fearful of losing power and control. "How dare the peasants make up policy!" Some of the greatest suggestions and ideas within law enforcement have been created by the crusty 25-year veteran just doing his/her job. They have no ambition or alternative motive in their suggestions. The only motive they have is to get the job done, do the job efficiently, and go home at the end of the shift. That's it! No bullshit, no filler, and no memorandums that take four months for approval to attack a crime trend that'll be over by the time it's approved.

I shit you not true story. In my old agency, everything was a "memo". When I was a Sergeant we also had a large spike of crime during spring break. The crimes were robberies, larceny from auto's, and other nuisance crimes. The plan was to do "Operation Spring Break". In my department true fashion, I was requested to complete a memorandum and pass it up the chain. I made this memorandum like a Michaelangelo masterpiece. I put graphs and fiscal analysis which commanders love. They like pretty simple pop up's. I passed this memorandum up the chain in February for execution in late March. July I got my memorandum back rejected. The deputy chief's reasoning was that if we went into these communities our presence and proactive policing would cause our crime number to spike. Think about that.. Our whole mission as law enforcement is to catch criminals and protect the citizens.

This deputy chief is now the Chief of Police in my old agency. Exactly what I spoke about before rings true. We reward bad leadership with better positions. We can't break out of the cycle of giving commanders that have been commanders for more time than they served on the street higher positions. We have commanders that spent five years as patrol officers and 23-years in command positions.

When a Chief of Police job opens and national searches are conducted the resume with multiple chief jobs and bouncing from place to place is treated like that gold statue in Indiana Jones.

These Chiefs go into departments and do the "It'll work this time" move. The policies and bad decisions they made in their former agencies they bring to new agencies and give it another go. "It didn't work because of me, it didn't work because it was the agency". I've seen this time and time again.

Commanders and Chiefs of Police can only contribute to some of the reasons for our inner turmoil within law enforcement. I'd like to sit here all day and blame them but in fairness, we eat our own.

We do an absolutely terrible job helping each other. Before you throw this book across the room hear me out. When we hear an officer has been walked out or under investigation, what's the thing that everyone does? Yep, we all start speculating. We leave that officer hanging out in the cold. All communication is cut off to them and they are isolated. They are excommunicated from the agency until the higher-ups or Internal Investigations says "We smacked them around and they can come back to play".

This always perplexed me. If you got a call for a person on a bridge about to jump and get there and start to build a rapport with them, would you leave them? Would you walk off and start a coffee clutch and start talking about them while they cling to the bridge. Of course not. You're going to do everything in your power to stay with them and use every verbal skill you have to safely come off the ledge. Yet we don't even do that for our own brothers and sisters in distress. We automatically in some cases put them on trial, convict them, and dish punishment before they can even turn in their property and uniforms.

This is where we need to start and change the culture. We need to stop believing that Internal Investigations aren't politically motivated and the people in those positions hold biases.

Internal Investigations are antiquated and unreliable for the current times within law enforcement. The days of these investigations being conducted behind closed doors and cloak and dagger style of investigating needs to stop. The public has no idea how many internal investigations are bull shit or the ones that are legit are swept under the rug because the person is connected within the agency and belongs to the right "click".

Internal Investigations need to be taken out of the hand of the department and handled at the state level where the investigation is handled unbiased and with no loyalty to anyone within the agency. That's my hope one day but unfortunately unrealistic because of the power grab. In some cases, Chiefs use Internal Investigation as their own extermination unit. "It's not me, Internal Investigations did the investigation, I just dish out punishment".

Change the internal culture and then we have a shot at making our profession amazing again.

Samantha Smith

I can remember the moment like it was yesterday, I was nervously waiting by the phone, as it felt like time was not moving. You know when you are extra hungry and you keep opening the same fridge door thinking something will suddenly appear that you want; that is essentially what I was doing by refreshing my phone a million times. I had applied to several local city departments and I knew the call would be coming soon to let me know if I was being offered the job. The phone eventually rang and I was offered the job with a decent size city department in Northern VA. Fast forward to the first day of the Police Academy, after getting dropped into pushup position in my dress clothes and getting yelled out, we were brought inside a large room for an afternoon of speakers. I recall the Director of the academy welcoming us, and although he said many things I no longer remember, one thing stuck with me. The Director said that we were now a part of the blue family, and even though we all come from different families and backgrounds, different cities, and past experiences, we were now all together with thousands of other brothers and sisters of blue across the World. Those words rang impacted me greatly, as I always wanted to feel a part of something larger than myself. To feel like I was making a positive impact, but also that I have other like-minded people by my side fighting for the same cause. It was us versus them, good versus evil, standing together to form the thin blue line against the chaos of the World. Or so I thought.

It all started when I graduated from the academy and began my field training phase (FTO). For 6 months I was the "newbie" and those more senior to me made sure to let me know. Most were supportive and helpful as I learned, but you could tell patience was thin amongst the ranks for us new Officers as these senior members were already stretched thin. Between running from call to call, dealing with citizens on their worst days, and then having to defend themselves against the upper brass, the last thing these senior officers wanted was a newcomer asking a million questions or needing their handheld to do their job. We felt more like a burden to them than as if we were a part of the solution. It was not our fault either; while the academy prepared us well, those 6 months went out the window the first time our boots hit the ground. Everything I learned about being a cop, I learned on the street interacting with the community I served. The divide amongst the ranks was clear from day one, and to make matters worse, there was inner turmoil amongst the shifts and cliches. It was hard trying to fit in and find a place to be accepted and valued as a member of the family. I remember the Director saying, these are my brothers and sisters and I would shake my head thinking maybe he was right, but I was just misunderstanding his words. Maybe, he meant like a good rivalry amongst siblings that we often see in households, with name-calling, tattle-telling, and beating each other when the boss of the home looks away. It was beginning to seem like it was not us versus them meaning the cops versus the bad guys in society; rather, it was us versus them, standing side by side on the thin blue line, pushing each other down and climbing on one another to get to the next better spot in line.

I always knew getting into law enforcement as a female I would have to work harder to prove myself. While I do not agree with this mentality, I accepted it as the way things were within Law Enforcement. Whenever I would be assigned to a new shift, I would have to start all over again. The guys would look at me and roll their eyes, just like they did my entire life. I can recall growing up being the only girl in the all-boys baseball league. Yes, league, not team! I would step up to bat and the pitcher would yell, "it's a girl, move in she won't hit it far." I would dig my cleats into the dirt and grip the bat as hard as I could as I took a swing with all my might and the ball would fly over their heads. As I would round the bases, I would giggle to myself as I felt I was teaching them a lesson to not underestimate a girl. Those same feelings would arise as I would meet the new group of Officers. I would keep my head down and go about my business as the assignments were called out. I would realize quickly that the guys who joined the shift as new members would immediately be considered "one of the guys," while I was left on the sidelines trying to figure out my way in. It took me a few weeks until I figured it out. It was my first call with a combative subject. We had to go hands-on and ended up rolling around in the dirt fighting the subject to get them under control and into cuffs. After that call, I was suddenly treated differently. I was being invited to window up with the guys, grab lunch together even get together after a shift to hang out. You see, for the guys they assumed since I was a woman I would not be able to handle myself. It was not until I "proved" myself that I was fully accepted. Unfortunately, this mentality of judging upon gender was a fallacy, just as it was on the baseball field. My gender did not influence my ability to do the job, heck I have seen men larger in size than me who could not handle themselves when faced with a combative subject. Once again, my blue family was creating a divide from within that was not warranted. This was not what was supposed to happen, my brothers were supposed to have my back and accept me just as they did the other guys. At the end of the day, I wore the same uniform and badge as they did.

The divide amongst my blue family only heightened when I became a Crisis Intervention Officer (CIT). So many of my counterparts were against the CIT program saying it was the "hug a thug" program. Having grown up in a family knowing mental health and the effects it has on people of all walks of life, I was enraged by this saying. The CIT program was implemented to ensure the Police Department has trained officers to handle critical incidents with citizens who often were dealing with a mental health crisis.

We were trained on how to handle suicidal individuals, schizophrenic episodes, and much more. I remember in the training, one day we were instructed to place headphones on, as soon as we did numerous random voices would begin playing on repeat with horrible derogatory rhetoric that was overwhelming in different tones and pitches. All while this was occurring, we were instructed to visit the fake supermarket the trainers set up with our monopoly money check out specific items and get our change. This scenario taught us what it feels like for someone who hears internal voices. It made the simplest everyday task that we take for granted, seem impossible. Counting money or trying to focus on directions was intense and almost all of us became abundantly frustrated within a few minutes we're grateful to be able to remove the headphones. For one to truly understand what someone with a mental health crisis is experiencing, we must learn empathy and compassion before anything else. For many within the blue family, this creates a divide amongst the siblings as those who support and wanted to be CIT trained were seen as soft or weak. This unfortunately spilled over into our everyday life as Officers.

I'll never forget the call, and not because it was the worst one I dealt with, or because it was a close call; rather, because it solidified my concern that we are not supporting each other in this blue family. We are aiding in killing each other within the ranks as we do not support one another when it matters most. It was one thing to be a part of the CIT team and for Officers to snark and make comments about being a soft officer, but it was another when those officers would refuse to be there for you in your dark moments. I was on phase 2 of my FTO program when we were dispatched to a home for a fall victim. The individual a man in his early 20's had fallen in the bathroom and needed help. I recall thinking to myself as we were dispatched, why would a young 20-year-old man need help to lift himself.

As we arrived on the scene, my FTO and I approached the apartment door and let ourselves in announcing we were on site. I remember seeing beautiful pictures of a wedding with a happy smiling couple surrounded by loving friends and family. The apartment was well kept and it smelled like a fresh candle had just been lit. All of this further confused me as we walked inside because most lift-assist or fall calls I had been on usually were for older individuals, and the homes were chaotic and often did not smell the greatest. We turned the corner and I saw a walker on its side, along with the young man lying on the ground. He was alert and responsive, as he began answering my FTO's questions. For me, I froze. Yes, froze. Right there in the hallway looking down at what I thought was supposed to be a young man in his early 20's, instead, my eyes were looking at a frail body that appeared to be in his 50's or 60's. His bones were protruding underneath his thin skin filled with bruising and discoloration consistent with an elderly sick person. His cheeks were sunken in and his eyes discolored. He spoke softly as if every word was a battle to produce and was simply trying to survive. I was snapped out of my frozen stupor by the Fire Department arriving on the scene. I moved out of the way to allow them in and they quickly lifted him and helped him sit on the couch. They called him by his first name and it was evident they had visited this location multiple times. As the EMTs began checking his vitals, my eyes wandered to those Wedding pictures again and I realized why I was so confused. That man lying on the ground truly was in his early 20's, but his body was decaying from the inside out, as he fought a disease. He was not in his 50s or 60s, he was not elderly and had lived a long and happy life, he was my age! He was just starting out, recently married to his best friend, and within just a few short months, now fighting for his life. His wife was a nurse at the nearby hospital and was rushing back home while the EMTs checked him to be by his side and support him.

This was far from the worst scene I had seen up to this point in my Law Enforcement career, but this one hit me differently. I realized this could have been me, I mean we were the exact same age and this young man was fighting to survive, unable to even lift himself from the ground or answer a few questions without needing supplemental oxygen. I was not naive to know young people die sometimes, but seeing up close this man's struggle hit home for me. I felt the emotions welling over, I was no longer frozen and confused; rather, I was feeling every sensation in my body. My heart was racing, I felt the sweat beginning to pool on my forehead and my legs felt a bit rubbery. I wanted to escape these feelings to run away and unsee what I had just witnessed. I wanted to forget that death does not discriminate against age or the fact that he was recently married and just starting his life. I found myself in the hallway trying to catch my breath. My bulletproof vest felt heavier and more constricting than earlier in the day, I felt like I was being crushed from all 4 walls and needed to escape. I yelled to my FTO that I was stepping outside and ran down the stair, out to the patrol unit, and sat down with the window open.

The cool air brushing against my face helped to bring me back to reality a bit. Within a few moments and a few deep breaths I felt myself calming a bit as I thought to myself, I can just wait here and do not need to go back inside. Thankfully, my hopes of not returning were granted when my FTO exited as the EMTs wheeled the young man on the stretcher into the back of the ambulance. My FTO got in the vehicle and I sighed in relief as the worst was over, but I was wrong. As I sat in the vehicle, I was waiting for my FTO to ask me about the call, to allow me to work through my racing thoughts and emotions, instead I received nothing. I was hoping to gain insight from my senior trainer on how to deal with things when they hit close to home or resonate with you. Instead, my FTO immediately opened his phone and started yelling about the current baseball game that was on, and at that moment I realized I was all alone. My emotions and thoughts, my racing heart, and weak legs were not felt by my Brother in blue, rather I was in my own battle. At that moment I needed to be seen and heard. I needed to express and question and feel safe, but none of that occurred. Many years later when an injury eventually took me out of Law

Enforcement, I realized that as much as I loved and supported the CIT program for the citizens we served, we also needed a program that would support our blue family from within. That call I experienced shook me and I remember driving home from shift crying that evening. I never spoke to anyone about it, because I feared judgment and embarrassment. It did not feel safe to express my vulnerabilities as an empathetic officer, rather I needed to be like my FTO and simply move on. The truth is, I do not think we ever truly move on, we just learn to compartmentalize. We shove those scenes, those moments, those calls into a box and lock away the key. Our blue family does not ever hear about them, sometimes until it is too late. Now, I do not blame my FTO for they did not impose those feelings of judgment and embarrassment on me, but if we are not purposely looking out for each other even after what seems like a "routine" call, then who will? At the end of the day, isn't that what family is for?

My blue family became further divided when I relocated to South Texas and joined a smaller suburban department. I was the only Woman on patrol, heck I was the only Woman Officer except for a part-time reserve officer. There were no women in leadership, no diversity at all. Moreover, at this time in my life I was openly married to another woman, so let's add I was the first and only openly gay person to ever work for this department. This did not bother me as I enjoyed being able to help others see outside their box. Sometimes, it takes a person getting to know someone who is different from them to gain some acceptance and support. Plus, as the Director of the academy said years ago, I was a Sister in this blue family regardless of whom I was married to, or so I thought!

I was working midnights for a few months now with this new department when I found myself encountering an individual in the middle of the road around 2 am. The man was walking in circles in the road, completely disregarding the shining lights of my patrol car approaching him. I immediately radioed dispatch to mark me out with an unknown male at my location and to send me an additional unit. I briefly glanced at the patrol map and saw 2 of my units were next to each other not too far from me, so I knew backup would be there shortly. I activated my lights and pulled off to the side of the road. I exited my vehicle and shinned my flashlight near the individual. I spoke loudly trying to get his attention, but he did not respond to my voice or my lights. I approached a bit closer as I began to give verbal commands for him to step to the side of the street. As I approached, I realized this individual was either under the influence of a substance or possibly having a medical episode causing him to have a distorted ability to see and hear me. Eventually, after several more loud commands, I was able to get his attention and he walked to the side of the street. I had him take a seat next to the patrol vehicle where I could wait for my backup and then determine our next steps to safely proceed. I began asking him some simple questions to ascertain his name and address, maybe a phone number or someone we could call to get some more information. All the while, I began to realize it seemed like my backup was taking a long time to arrive. As I continued to stall by asking questions, I knew something was wrong with my backup, but I could not go into my vehicle to see the map as I needed to stay with the individual. I was about to radio my dispatch and ask for an ETA when I saw the red and blues turn the corner.

The cruiser parked behind mine, but I was surprised to see a dark-colored uniform exit the unit with our neighboring city patch on the sleeve. The Officer said he overheard me mark out and did not hear backup arrive on the scene so he headed my way. I thanked him for coming to back me up and he assisted me in ultimately locating the individual's Mother, who explained he had a medical condition that caused him to get disoriented sometimes. She was able to make our location and return him safely home. I was walking back to my unit when the other officer mentioned it was odd that my guys never showed, to which I made some silly excuse and brushed it off. I thanked him again and he drove away, as I sat in my unit wondering what just happened. I covered for my Brothers, just as I did as a young child for my own brother if he did something wrong. As I sat there trying to piece it all together, I looked at the map on my screen and noticed that the two units were in the exact same spot they were when I marked out several minutes ago. They had never moved, they were never coming to back me up, once again I was alone as an Officer with no support from my blue family.

As I often did on my midnight tours, I wrote an email to my Wife to express what happened since I did not want to wake her. I told her I was confused, hurt, scared, and felt alone. I wrote that maybe they were tied up with something, maybe they were on a special assignment I was unaware of. I was making excuses up for them when they did not deserve them. As my shift ended, I returned to the station and realized what happened that night. The news was on in the roll call room speaking about politics and the LGBT+ community, and the comments they were making and the giggles that followed made it abundantly clear that I lived a life as an out Lesbian to which they did not agree. I ultimately was moved to another shift shortly after that incident and while I still had to see those guys every once in a while, I was happy to be on a shift where my guys had my back as I had theirs. I never thought that the person I love and was married to would drive my fellow blue family to not have my back.

Again, we wore the same uniform and badge, we went into the same dangerous situations with the goal of going home at night, but for them, I was different an outcast, and one who did not deserve the support of my family.

Unfortunately, I was mistaken and realized that we were tearing each other down, putting each other at risk, and ultimately killing each other from within the ranks for the department.

Jumping ahead to the present day, I see things a bit differently. I am grateful for the time I served and the skills I learned. I am honored to have saved a life, left a positive impact on the community, and been a part of the great good for the citizens I served. My back injury was a blessing in disguise as it took away my dream of being an Officer for the rest of my life, but it allowed me to now support the Law Enforcement community differently. Further, I ended up becoming a hose dragger (inside cop joke) and volunteering with a local Fire Department. My back eventually ruined that for the long term, but now I get to recruit others to begin their career path in being a first responder with the Fire Service.

My blood will always bleed a little bit of blue, and some red now for the fire service and heck even a little rainbow for my LGBT+ community, but at the end of the day, regardless of the uniform being worn, I am willing to continue that hard work that is needed to support every person as they are. Sometimes that looks like speaking out, sometimes it looks like listening better to a fellow first responder in their darkness but, ultimately when our family is unable to provide the support we need, we must put ourselves in positions to make the positive change from within. We ARE first responders, we fight and don't give up, so let's do just that; but, instead of against each other, let's remember how we stand on that thin blue line together for the greater good!

Now I get it, some of you reading this are probably thinking that this all sounds wonderful in theory, but how does it translate to you and where you are. Whether you are in Law Enforcement or not, the same applies. We as a collective community have to be willing to identify and admit when there is a problem, be willing to step up and stand tall to effect the change that is needed, and ultimately see the bigger picture. This looks like being vulnerable. Ah, a word almost every Cop despises! Being vulnerable means admitting when a call hits hard, calling out our blue brothers and sisters when a fellow Officer or Commander does something wrong, asking for help and support in those dark moments, and demanding equality within the family regardless of rank. This level of vulnerability is displayed in everything you read from Nick and me because I promise you it is not easy to be open and honest with those stories we shared, but it is necessary. That level of vulnerability is not weak or soft, rather is it courageous and strong. The equation is simple, vulnerability = Courage = YOUR voice be heard! We must be vulnerable, in order to be courageous to ensure our voices are heard! This goes to all of us, whether a citizen or a first responder, the same applies. So be VULNERABLE, be COURAGEOUS and make sure YOUR VOICE IS HEARD!

www.ingramcontent.com/pod-product-compliance
Lightning Source LLC
Chambersburg PA
CBHW030453220526
45464CB00006B/2519